To:

_____

From:

_____

Message:

_____

_____

_____

_____

LOSING A
Loved One

CHRISTIAN ART
PUBLISHERS

Published by Christian Art Publishers,
PO Box 1599, Vereeniging, 1930

© 2023
First edition 2023

Originally published in Afrikaans under the title *Wanneer 'n geliefde sterf*
Translated by Therina van der Westhuizen

Cover designed by Christian Art Publishers
Designed by Christian Art Publishers
Images used under license from Shutterstock.com

Scripture quotations are taken from the Holy Bible, New International Version® NIV®.
Copyright © 1973, 1978, 1984, 2011 by International Bible Society.
Used by permission of Biblica, Inc.® All rights reserved worldwide.

Scripture quotations are taken from the Holy Bible, New Living Translation,
copyright © 1996, 2004, 2015 by Tyndale House Foundation.
Used by permission of Tyndale House Publishers, Inc., Carol Stream, Illinois 60188.
All rights reserved.

Printed in China

ISBN 978-0-638-00054-2

24   25   26   27   28   29   30   31   32   33   –   11   10   9   8   7   6   5   4   3   2

Introduction

When a loved one dies, your whole world comes to a standstill. It feels like there is no way that it could actually be true. It seems unthinkable to carry on with your life without that person in it. The pain and sadness are unbearable.

It really is unthinkable and even impossible to carry that burden alone. God is the only One who makes it bearable, step by step, day by day, sometimes even minute by minute. This book aims to help you walk this painful path with God. He promises to remain close by and to surround you with His presence every single moment. Sadly, in a time of sorrow it is often hard to experience His presence. This book will help you become more aware of it and understand God better.

Read it somewhere quiet and peaceful. Even if you do not feel at peace right now, the gift of peace will return to your life. You will soon feel the words of Saint Augustine ring true for you too: "O Lord, our heart is restless until it finds its rest in You."

This book is a journey, one that you must complete despite the pain of mourning and sorrow. For most of us this journey is unknown, because even if you have lost a loved one in the past, every journey is different.

There are, however, two things you can be sure of in this journey. The first is that your journey is already underway. As soon as you get the news of a loved one's passing, you set off on your journey. The second is that you are not alone—Jesus travels with you. That is what He promised to do and He always keeps His promises. At times it may seem as though He is far away but remember that is just a feeling and feelings are not facts.

There are many uncertainties along this journey. How long will it take? Will I spend the entire time in the wilderness or will I at least find an oasis somewhere? Will my other loved ones travel with me or will we sometimes lose each other along the way? Will it become more bearable or will it always be this intensely painful?

This book contains 40 devotions. In the Bible, the number 40 is often used symbolically to indicate a time of completion. There is certainly no expectation for you to complete your journey of mourning in 40 days. The only answer is to keep going. When we experience great sorrow, it is best not to look too far ahead, but rather to keep moving forward step by step, hour by hour. As you continue on your journey, the answers will become clearer.

May you experience the Lord beside you, in front of you, around you, above you and in you.

– Henk Gous

The Lord
is *close* to
the brokenhearted
and *saves* those
who are crushed in spirit.
Psalm 34:18

Feed
Your Soul

In our times of sorrow
we find food for the soul
that nourishes the bones
and marrow of our faith
in ways that would not
happen otherwise.
Eat this food.
As long as God keeps
you in the season of sorrow,
do not waste it by wishing
the time away.
Eat the fruit that only grow
on the tree of sorrow.

– John Piper

1

Endless Tears

Be merciful to me, LORD, for I am in distress;
my eyes grow weak with sorrow,
my soul and body with grief. (Psalm 31:9 NIV)

*I*t is impossible to sleep that first night after a loved one's passing. Your thoughts run wild and it seems impossible to switch them off. The only thing that finally makes you fall asleep is absolute exhaustion. You are tired of crying. Your face is tender and red from wiping away all the tears and blowing your nose. You feel weak, just like Psalm 31 describes.

Love is what makes you cry until there is nothing left. It would have been so much better had it been an acquaintance or someone you hadn't heard from in a long time. That is the price of love; the risk of loving someone intensely. That is why every tear you've shed and will still shed is worth it. Your loved one deserves your tears—all of them. So, don't be afraid to cry.

Being capable of this extraordinary emotion we know as love is all part of Jesus' plan. His plan entails feeling like you're on cloud nine when you find love, and feeling shattered when you lose love. Thankfully, He gives us His grace whenever we lose love. The cure to this first day of constant crying is His grace—His unshakable love that is always with us (Psalm 32:10). Even when you feel like you're all alone with only a blanket to comfort you, remember that God's loving arms are always around you.

It can be therapeutic to write down all the thoughts and emotions you are experiencing. Don't worry about good grammar or arranging it in a logical order. Writing in this way helps to calm your heart. That is why these 40 devotions offer you a space to pen down your feelings, to clear your mind. Write until you can't write anymore.

Write down everything that's on your heart today.

_____

_____

_____

_____

_____

_____

_____

_____

_____

_____

_____

_____

_____

Lord, today I don't have much to say. I am tired of crying and talking to so many people. I am struggling to come to terms with what happened. Please help me. Amen.

2

Jesus Cries with You

*When Jesus saw her weeping, and the Jews who
had come along with her also weeping, He was deeply
moved in spirit and troubled. Jesus wept. Jesus, once more
deeply moved, came to the tomb. It was a cave with
a stone laid across the entrance. (John 11:33, 35, 38 NIV)*

Have you ever wondered why Jesus cried here? After all, He knew that He was going to resurrect Lazarus, so why did He cry? It makes sense that the other people were crying because in their mind, Lazarus was dead and would stay dead.

Jesus cried here because He shared Martha and Mary's sorrow. He truly felt it with them. People often say, "We are mourning with you," especially now when they come to visit you to offer their condolences. But we know that isn't always true. It is very difficult to truly share in another person's pain.

It is, however, something that Jesus is able to do—then and now. When everyone has left and you just want to sit and cry, Jesus will sit next to you and cry with you. He certainly has all the answers and solutions, but He will give those to you later. For now, all He offers is His loving presence and genuine compassion.

Just sit or lie with Jesus.

He does not scold you for crying; instead, He helps you to dry your tears.

Write down how it makes you feel to know that Jesus is with you and that He is ready to dry your tears.

_____

_____

_____

_____

_____

_____

_____

_____

_____

_____

_____

_____

_____

_____

_____

_____

_____

_____

_____

_____

Heavenly Father, thank You for going to Martha and Mary. You had such love and compassion for them. All I ask is that You will stay with me today and hold me close. Amen.

3

You Can Go to Jesus

Suddenly, a fierce storm struck the lake, with waves
breaking into the boat. But Jesus was sleeping.
The disciples went and woke Him up, shouting,
"Lord, save us! We're going to drown!" (Matthew 8:24-25 NLT)

Alarm systems have two main functions: They make you aware that there is an emergency, and serve as a cry for help. The storm on the lake served as an alarm for the disciples. They suddenly realized that the emergency was too great for them to handle. The storm was a matter of life or death. And that is when they finally called for help.

We know that we need God's help every waking moment. But often we only ask for help once things have become totally unbearable. Perhaps we mean well and don't want to shift all our responsibility onto God, expecting Him to sort out every little thing. Perhaps we just don't want to bother Him, or we don't want to admit that we can't go on anymore.

You may, however, cry out to the Lord. You may constantly ask Him to help you cope with your anxiety about tomorrow's loneliness. Then Jesus will explain to you that you do not need to fret because He is always with you. After that, He will deal with the storm. Jesus calmed the storm on the lake, and demonstrated that He is God and He is able.

Today's storm of sorrow may not subside all at once, but eventually it will because He is the One who can still any storm.

Write down everything that you want to take to Jesus today.

_____

_____

_____

_____

_____

_____

_____

_____

_____

_____

_____

_____

_____

_____

_____

_____

_____

_____

_____

_____

Prince of peace, I am very familiar with the story of the storm. I would have woken You up a lot sooner than the disciples did. I am going to keep crying out to You, because this storm I am in is very bad. Lord, save me! Because it feels like I am going to drown! Amen.

4

No Time for Goodbyes

Early on the first day of the week, while it was still dark,
Mary Magdalene went to the tomb and saw that the stone
had been removed from the entrance. (John 20:1 NIV)

Why did Mary Magdalene visit the grave even before the sun was out? Because she did not get a chance to say goodbye to Jesus before He died. Even though it was too late to say goodbye now, she still had that burning desire in her heart to bid Him farewell. It is very difficult but also very healing, to be by someone's side during their final moments. You are able to hold their hand. You can speak comforting words, even though your loved one may no longer be able to hear you. Everyone can grieve together and say goodbye. It may also help you to come to terms with the reality that your loved one has truly passed away.

At Jesus' burial, His loved ones were driven away from the cross and other "undertakers" buried Him—they gave Him a proper burial but without His loved ones there. If that is how you had to part with your loved one, it may be especially hard on you because you weren't able to experience that precious goodbye. There may be so much that you left unsaid. Jesus is the only One who can help you. Go ahead and tell Him those things that you wanted to say to your loved one—He will convey the message. Or write it in a letter to your loved one, which you can read out loud. Go ahead and do it, it can be very healing.

If you had the opportunity, what would you want to say to your loved one?

_____

_____

_____

_____

_____

_____

_____

_____

_____

_____

_____

_____

_____

_____

_____

_____

_____

_____

_____

Lord, I did not have the chance to say goodbye. I really wish that I could have said more, that my loved one could have heard more. But, Lord, You know the words echoing in my heart. Thank You that I can tell You all the things that I still wanted to say. Thank You for understanding. Amen.

5

David Loses It

*The king was overcome with emotion. He went up to
the room over the gateway and burst into tears.
And as he went, he cried, "O my son Absalom!
My son, my son Absalom! If only I had died instead
of you! O Absalom, my son, my son." Word soon
reached Joab that the king was weeping and
mourning for Absalom. (2 Samuel 18:33—19:1 NLT)*

The death of any loved one has an enormous impact on us. In some cases, the impact is twofold because there is the pain of trauma as well as the pain of loss. If your young spouse or child dies, you lose your future. After a long marriage, you lose half of your entire existence. If your loved one dies in a violent manner, you lose faith in the goodness of a country.

In instances such as these, you need to have compassion for yourself—and others—because you understand the weight of the matter. If you lose a spouse or a child, the impact is enormous. And if a child loses a parent, the impact is equally big.

It is important to realize that David's conduct was actually "normal" even though everyone else thought that it made absolutely no sense. It is "normal" to feel excruciating pain. It is quite "normal" to feel that you may be losing your mind. The pain, loss and depression simply become too much to handle.

Who is going to keep you from falling apart? Only God and those He sends to help you. Tell Him about your anxiety. Tell your friends about all your confused thoughts and emotions. God's grace can put the broken pieces back together again.

What are the things you "lost" when your loved one died? A future? Security? Trust in God? Take all your emotions to Him.

Lord, You alone can calm me. You offer rest in my most turbulent times. Sometimes I am afraid that I might lose it completely. Please give me peace of mind. Send me friends to help me find clarity again. Amen.

6

Celebrate and Remember

LORD, You alone are my portion and my cup;
You make my lot secure. The boundary lines
have fallen for me in pleasant places; surely,
I have a delightful inheritance. (Psalm 16:5-6 NIV)

The main purpose of a funeral or memorial service is to remember, to honor. It is an opportunity to think back on the grace-filled times we were able to spend with our loved one. We can chat and reminisce and look at old photographs.

It is an ending where we can see the full life they lived. We can be grateful together because the measured-out portion of their life was filled with precious experiences. Of course, some parts were sad and even awful, but the grace of God can wash those instances in their life away and bring forgiveness. There is joy because despite all this, there is still so much to celebrate—years of life, friends and family, achievements…

It is like the areas of land the Israelites inherited in the Promised Land. Each received a specific area that covered beautiful and barren parts of the land. Your own inherited piece of land becomes the most beautiful farm if you choose to view it through a lens of gratitude, and you start sowing and reaping on it. Your memories are what make it beautiful. The same goes for your loved one's "inheritance".

What can you celebrate at the funeral? What are the special experiences that you and your loved one shared with others? Because the Lord is part of your inheritance and He "farmed" the land with you, the funeral can be a true celebration even though you are sad.

Write down all the things you remember about your loved one today. Whether you want to share it with others is entirely up to you.

Generous Father, today I looked through all Your gifts and we have received so many. There is so much to remember. Allow me to remember these things in the future with less pain and more joy. Also allow the plants of good memories to grow over and cover up the "stony" memories. Amen.

7

A Family Affair

A father to the fatherless, a defender of widows, is God
in His holy dwelling. God sets the lonely in families,
He leads out the prisoners with singing; but the
rebellious live in a sun-scorched land. (Psalm 68:5-6 NIV)

The vulnerability of widows and orphans in the olden days was unimaginable. When they lost a husband or a parent, they not only had to deal with the pain and longing for their loved one, but were also faced with a crisis of survival. They lost all their protection in society. They lost property and their means to survive because in those times they did not have things like pensions or life insurance. They were defenseless and could be exploited by anyone.

So, Psalm 68 served as an anchor for every widow and orphan. God will provide. God will, in His way and at the right time, offer security and ensure survival. He often did so by providing a new family. Their society heeded Jesus' instruction to be different from the societies around them: They were not to exploit the vulnerable but rather tasked to do everything in their power to protect them. The same instruction applies to us today—we ought to treat the most vulnerable like our own family, through practical support and love.

Therefore, a memorial service is a family affair. It is a time to embrace each other and support each other in love. Each person there is actually declaring their love. Have another look at everyone who attended. Those are the people God will use to care for you in your loneliness.

After the funeral, your feelings of loneliness may intensify. Write down how you feel now that everyone is gone.

_____

_____

_____

_____

_____

_____

_____

_____

_____

_____

_____

_____

_____

_____

_____

_____

_____

_____

_____

_____

Lord of love, this empty place makes me feel extremely lonely and vulnerable, because my soulmate is gone. So, I thank You for other people. Thank You for wrapping me in a blanket of meaningful relationships. I truly need those people in my life right now. Amen.

8

Finding Comfort

Jesus said to her, "I am the resurrection and the life.
The one who believes in Me will live,
even though they die; and whoever lives by
believing in Me will never die." (John 11:25-26 NIV)

When the funeral is focused solely on the past, it offers very little consolation. But when we look to the future together, it becomes an opportunity to find comfort. When we take Jesus' promise of resurrection and truly make it our own, we can comfort one another. That is the difference between people who believe in Christ and those who don't—we know that our human life does not end in death.

Without Jesus' promise of resurrection, death remains the most horrifying experience on earth. It is the absolute end, the tearing away of a loved one. It is irreversible and something we must accept as part of life.

However, Jesus changed death from being a final end to a gateway to something better. He not only made this promise to Martha and Mary in John 11, but also proved it when He resurrected Lazarus from the dead.

After the funeral, you will still feel sad and miss that person—you may even become impatient for the day to arrive when you will see each other again—but you will not be plagued by a fear of death.

Because we have accepted Jesus' death, resurrection and forgiveness, we are able to experience joy even amid sadness because one day we will spend eternity together in heaven.

Do you find comfort in knowing that death is merely a gateway and not the end? Describe what Jesus' promise of resurrection means to you.

_____

_____

_____

_____

_____

_____

_____

_____

_____

_____

_____

_____

_____

_____

_____

_____

_____

_____

Eternal God, thank You for eternity. I would not have been able to make it through this time without knowing that a wonderful reunion awaits us. Thank You for Jesus' resurrection that assures me of this. Amen.

A Special Place

*Moses, the servant of the Lord, died there in the land
of Moab, just as the Lord had said. The Lord buried
him in a valley near Beth-peor in Moab, but to this day
no one knows the exact place. (Deuteronomy 34:5-6 NLT)*

Many people need a place where they can feel close to their loved one. There are moments of intense longing. Where do you go in those times and does it really have to be a physical place? That body, which is now lifeless, was always your source of love. You were able to hold, feel and smell your loved one. Those are the things that you long for intensely now. There are indeed times when you experience your loved one close to you in your heart like when you visit a place that you went to together. Sometimes it is the smell of clothes, flowers or food that brings you comfort.

So do you really need a grave to find healing and comfort? Yes and no. A gravesite could offer healing if it is a place where you can reflect in peace and quiet, or where you can do something with your hands like placing a bunch of flowers or simply keeping the gravesite neat. But sometimes a grave is not necessary. Sometimes a single, simple gesture, like scattering their ashes in a meaningful place, can be enough. God did not think it necessary for Moses, the great leader, to have a visible gravesite. Maybe He did not want people to deface or even worship the grave.

Whether you visit the grave of a loved one or choose to scatter their ashes in a special place, ask Jesus to go with you. Let Him be your healing.

What can you do to feel close to your loved one? How important to you is a physical place where you can be close to your loved one?

Lord, I have a deep need and longing that I can't express in words. I just want to feel close to my loved one but all I have is a grave or an urn of ashes. Give me a sense of closeness in my heart today—a special place or a moment that I can cling to. Amen.

Job's Faith

*"The LORD gave me what I had, and the LORD
has taken it away. Praise the name of the LORD!"
In all of this, Job did not sin by blaming God. (Job 1:21-22 NLT)*

The disasters that hit Job in two short chapters were extreme, some might say unbearable. As if losing all his possessions was not bad enough, the death of all his children at once is indescribable and incomprehensible.

And yet he responds with unnatural calmness and extraordinary faith. He does not cry, he does not scream. But he does perform the mourning rituals of the time by tearing his clothes and shaving off all his hair. He does it so calmly that we are unable to comprehend it. People usually do not respond like that. Such trauma would surely make one cry at the very least, not so? How are we to interpret this?

Sometimes there is a sense of emotional numbness when you are in shock after losing a loved one. It is like being in some kind of haze, like the pain is being dulled by some "heavenly anesthetic". That is when your deepest words are spoken; and if you have been a believer all your life, like Job, you will speak words of faith.

Of course, this is not the end of the sad road that we are walking. And Job did seem to "lose" the calmness and faith-filled words later on. He grappled with God in many more chapters. But, most importantly, he regained the faith that he had apparently "lost" in the end.

Maybe that is what your first words were as well—full of faith. That is precious. Thank God for those first words and the initial numbing of the pain.

Describe how you are trying to process your own sadness. Are you grappling with God? Can you testify of "heavenly anesthetic" in your life?

_____

_____

_____

_____

_____

_____

_____

_____

_____

_____

_____

_____

_____

_____

_____

_____

_____

Great Comforter, I don't know whether I was calm or simply dead inside. It was unnatural. But thank You, I am unable to bear those intense emotions all the time. I really needed Your "heavenly anesthetic." Amen.

God's Arms around Me

Grief is like going through a tunnel—
and sometimes we wonder if we'll ever
come out the other end.
But God has not abandoned you,
and He wants to comfort you
and assure you that He is with you.
Jesus' words are true:
"Blessed are those who mourn,
for they will be comforted" (Matthew 5:4).

– Billy Graham

11

Job's Wife Was Angry

*His wife said to him, "Are you still maintaining
your integrity? Curse God and die!" He replied,
"You are talking like a foolish woman. Shall we accept
good from God, and not trouble?" (Job 2:9-10 NIV)*

Job's wife was not calm like her husband. Her pain made her angry. She fought with Job and with God. She wanted to curse and scream. And it is completely understandable. We, however, tend to think that her behavior is unacceptable. No-one may dare question God, right? What if He slays you for your rebellion?

That is why Job immediately reprimanded her. He did not comfort her. He chastised her, told her that she was a "foolish woman" and scolded her in his piety.

If Job's wife only knew God's Father-heart; knew how patiently He would keep speaking to Job later until Job calmed down in chapter 42. But they both thought that God was angry.

Do you also see Him like that? Do you think that you must always be strong and pious in His presence? When we are in pain, we can cry and complain to God, and even be angry.

Anger often masks other deeper emotions like pain, powerlessness, sadness or longing. Fortunately, our heavenly Father knows what makes His children "misbehave" at times so He holds His frustrated children close to Him without rebuking them.

Are you also angry at God? Write down all your anger-filled thoughts. Then take them all to God and allow Him to comfort and calm you.

_____

_____

_____

_____

_____

_____

_____

_____

_____

_____

_____

_____

_____

_____

_____

_____

_____

Father God, I got really angry today. I am ashamed of what I said, but that is how I felt. Thank You for allowing me the space to be angry. Help me to find my way back to You every time so that You can hold me and calm me down again. Amen.

Job's Honesty

"Oh, why give light to those in misery,
and life to those who are bitter?" (Job 3:20 NLT)

J ob's initial piety disappears and he becomes down in the dumps. Over the next 39 chapters, he expresses every intense emotion, which is quite understandable after all his troubles and the death of all his children. He did not demonstrate his usual patience, but became rather stubborn. In his grief, he started to reason with God and kept looking for answers.

No matter how persistently we moan and groan, God is patient with us, just like He was with Job. In fact, Jesus actually encourages us to remain persistent in asking, seeking and knocking, because then we shall find (Matthew 7:7-11).

Job was suffering and wanted to know whether God was still acting fairly towards him and whether God would remain a place of safety for him. But his friends kept insisting that Job himself should accept responsibility, that he was to blame for every disaster that hit him. That, of course, only exacerbated his pain.

Ultimately, God Himself spoke to Job. However, He offered no logical explanation; He merely revealed His goodness and majesty to Job. Job was able to find rest in that. He knew that he was safe in God's hands, even when he did not understand the bigger picture.

When a disaster seems to make no sense and the pain is unbearable, all you can do is turn to God—talk to Him over and over again. He promises to listen patiently.

How comforting to know that we can open our hearts to God and keep asking until we understand. Write down all the questions you have for God and then take it to Him in prayer.

_____

_____

_____

_____

_____

_____

_____

_____

_____

_____

_____

_____

_____

_____

_____

_____

_____

_____

Dear Lord, I don't really understand the Book of Job. But I do understand one thing: Job's honesty. He was able to say and ask everything he wanted to. Thank You that I, too, can speak so openly and often to You. Amen.

13

Job Finds Rest

My ears had heard of You but now
my eyes have seen You. (Job 42:5 NIV)

You may be unable to imagine that your pain will ever subside. Job surely didn't think that he would be able to work through all his grief and suffering. And yet, here in chapter 42, he testified with certainty that he had seen God with his own eyes.

Job's first three friends were not very good helpers. They had only one answer for all his suffering: everything was his own fault. Fortunately, people's answers are not God's answers. In the end, God Himself spoke and He reminded Job of His greatness and of the vast creation that He continually maintains.

When Job looked, he found peace without getting answers. And then Job admitted that he had finally gotten to know God for who He really is. Only then was Job finally able to speak directly to God rather than about Him.

Is knowing just the basics enough for you? Or do you want all the answers so that you know everything? The crux of the matter is that God is our loving, almighty and caring Father. When the child is unable to understand everything, the Father only explains the basics. And even though that is not everything, we know that it is enough.

Write down what your friends are telling you in an attempt to help you. Ask God to help you consider everything that is positive and relevant.

_____

_____

_____

_____

_____

_____

_____

_____

_____

_____

_____

_____

_____

_____

_____

_____

_____

_____

My Father in heaven, I still have so many questions. I have spoken to many of my friends in order to find answers. Help me to hear Your voice, because You alone will give me the right answers. Amen.

14

Chest Pain

*You turned my wailing into dancing; You removed
my sackcloth and clothed me with joy. (Psalm 30:11 NIV)*

The pain of losing a loved one can be described as a burning arrow inside you. It is a pain only the Lord truly knows. Where has that arrow of pain lodged in you? The word "sadness" falls far short. It is much rather a searing pain in the heart. It is unabated grief. What are you supposed to do about it?

There is no quick fix. If you drink something to numb the pain, it could become a problem very quickly. We have no choice but to walk that long road with our Healer. He is the Tailor who takes off your sackcloth of mourning and convinces you over time that a garment of joy does suit you better. But how do we find this road?

Maybe the answer lies in the word "dance". When your body moves, something in your heart and mind changes as well. Exercise and movement can heal our painful thoughts. Even if you just get out of bed to go for a short stroll, it could help to numb the pain a little. Movement and exercise can help you to get rid of the sadness; you can sweat it out and later get rid of it completely.

Dancing is certainly contradictory to the feeling of sadness and you will surely need to force yourself to do it. But in the end, the Lord will restore your joy so that you will want to dance. That is His promise and miracle: Somewhere in the future, you will want to dance with joy again.

Write down a few ways in which you can be more active. It does not have to be anything drastic, just something to get you moving. And then go ahead and do it.

_____

_____

_____

_____

_____

_____

_____

_____

_____

_____

_____

_____

_____

_____

_____

_____

Lord, the sadness is so overwhelming that it feels as if every fiber of my being is in pain. Help me to hold on to the thought that You will restore my joy, that the intense pain will subside even if it does not feel like it right now. Give me Your joy. Amen.

15

Handling Grief

*By the rivers of Babylon we sat and wept when we
remembered Zion. Happy is the one who seizes your
infants and dashes them against the rocks. (Psalm 137:1, 9 NIV)*

*I*t is astonishing to think that tears could end in such cruelty. That is what happened when the Israelites were captives in Babylon and handled their grief the wrong way. As captives they had suffered enormous losses—they lost their home country and certainly lost loved ones as well. They were overwhelmed by grief and suffering. They found themselves in a beautiful place next to a beautiful river, but opted to cry rather than sing, which led to words of anger and revenge spilling out of them. How does that happen? Sadness, powerlessness and longing are best expressed through tears and words—it is healthy. An unhealthy way to give vent to one's feelings is through anger. But anger happens: In my grief I sometimes beat against the bed with my fist, or I spewed angry words. Our bottled-up emotions are so strong that we fight with one another. So what now?

If the Israelites had not hung up their harps and stopped singing, their anger may have been less severe. When you express your emotions through words they become less severe. The sadness will become less of a bottled-up force threatening to explode in an outburst of anger. The next time you feel like you are going to have an outburst, use God's gift of music. Look for music that you can cry to, but that will also comfort you.

It's normal to be angry. You must take your anger to God and ask Him to comfort you. Which song offers you comfort? Maybe "Nearer, My God, To Thee" or "Amazing Grace"? Write down the lyrics of your heart's song below.

_____

_____

_____

_____

_____

_____

_____

_____

_____

_____

_____

_____

_____

_____

_____

Lord, I am angry and confused. And sometimes, it has been easier to blame You. But You surprised me with Your response. You did not rebuke me or tell me to be quiet. You forgave me and offered me understanding. You held me closer and comforted me. Now I realize that I was only powerless and grief-ridden. You helped me once more. Amen.

16

A Steep Road

The Sovereign LORD is my strength; He makes
my feet like the feet of a deer, He enables me
to tread on the heights. (Habakkuk 3:19 NIV)

When we go on holiday, we always plan our route as carefully as possible. If you drive an ordinary sedan, you will, for instance, not select a 4x4 route. Sometimes, however, we do end up on an unplanned and difficult road with no way of turning around and then the only option we have is to continue on.

That is what happens when you lose a loved one. You suddenly find yourself on an impossibly difficult route. It is as if the highway of life suddenly comes to an end and you are confronted with the most difficult mountain pass ever. The following thoughts race through your mind, "But I can't do it. I am not ready for this. I am just an ordinary, little car that will break down on this road."

There is a wonderful promise in Habakkuk 3:19, namely, the Lord will give you entirely different treads on your tires for this seemingly impossible road ahead. Those treads are like the feet of a deer that can withstand the hard rocks, which will make your poor feet bleed. The Lord changes you. You may have thought that you are no more than a city car, but He suddenly transforms you into a sturdy 4x4 vehicle. He gives you the ability to reach the top.

If your past makes you think that you are too weak for what lies ahead, think again. Look at your feet, they are like a deer's. Are you ready to tackle this mountain pass with God's help? Then tomorrow will seem less impossible.

In which ways has the Lord strengthened you thus far to help you along your mountain pass route? Write your experience down here.

_____

_____

_____

_____

_____

_____

_____

_____

_____

_____

_____

_____

_____

_____

_____

_____

_____

_____

Lord, I look ahead and I realize that it is impossible for me go over these mountain passes. So, please change me. I feel weak and have no experience in scaling mountains. I need the feet of a deer. I know Your miracles are enough to ensure that I tread securely on the heights. Amen.

Moving On

*They will be like a vine whose grapes are harvested
too early, like an olive tree that loses its blossoms
before the fruit can form. (Job 15:33 NLT)*

People today are impatient. But those who know anything about nature also know that you cannot force something to become riper quicker. Neither can you interfere with the seasons of nature. You must wait patiently for things to ripen in their own time.

Grieving people are often confronted by impatient people. They may hear from those around them that they must stop mourning and move on. When is the right time to move on and carry on with your life after such an immense loss? Is there such a thing as the "right time"? There is no fixed time. There comes a time, however, when it has fully ripened. That is when enough time has passed and enough work has been put in for it to be ripe.

The right time, or when the time is ripe, lies somewhere between too short and too long. When you flee your mourning by making drastic decisions or living in denial, you are not giving yourself enough time. But it is also unhealthy for you to freeze and remain exactly the same for years.

Always remember that God is the One who ripens all fruit. While you keep talking to God, crying to Jesus and asking for wisdom from the Holy Spirit, things will gradually start to change—almost as inconspicuously as the ripening process.

Pray today to the God of the harvest and ask Him to ensure that there will be ripe fruit at the right time to harvest.

How far have you progressed on your journey of mourning? Write down all the things that you have not yet had the guts to do. Ask the Lord to guide you through them, one by one, when the time is right.

Dear Lord, I know life goes on but I don't want to. I am confused—sometimes I just want to throw away every little thing that reminds me of my loved one. At other times, I don't want to disturb a thing. You alone can help me to become ripe, to do the right things at the right time. Give me the courage to keep taking one step at a time. Amen.

Miserable Comforters

*Then Job replied: "I have heard many things like these;
you are miserable comforters, all of you! Will your
long-winded speeches never end?" (Job 16:1-3 NIV)*

Many people will come to see you to offer their condolences. And while some visits are very comforting, others are simply a burden.

M. Baylie writes: "Someone came to 'sympathize' with me. He told me that God has a purpose with everything. He didn't stop talking. Most of what he said I already knew and believed to be true. But all I wanted was for him to leave. Then someone else came and sat next to me. She did not speak. She just sat there next to me. When I said something, she listened attentively, gave a short reply, prayed a simple prayer, got up and left. It touched me deeply. I felt comforted. I was really sorry that she had to leave."

Treat each visitor with kindness. They only want to help. They will give you what they think you need at this time although very few of them know what you really need at this stage of your mourning journey. So, tell them what you need. Ask them to just listen, read the Bible with you, or make you a nice cup of tea. Ask them to give you some space, but also to be available when you might not want to be alone.

Sometimes, love is best expressed in mere silence and closeness. That's exactly what God is like, too.

It is true that some people's consolation means more than other's. Write down the names of all the people who supported you during this time—even if the consolation they had to offer was not quite what you needed at the time.

_____

_____

_____

_____

_____

_____

_____

_____

_____

_____

_____

_____

_____

_____

_____

_____

Dear Lord, please help my friends. Some of them mean really well, but are of no help to me at all. Please help me to ask them tactfully to change their approach. Thank You for all the special helpers who give me what I need right now. I would not be able to make it without them. Amen.

19

No Painkillers

Then they offered Him wine mixed with myrrh,
but He did not take it. (Mark 15:23 NIV)

Have you ever wondered why Jesus did not drink the wine mixed with myrrh that was offered to Him at His crucifixion? The reason was that the mixture is meant to numb the pain. Jesus chose to endure the pain while fully conscious and without any painkillers.

Sometimes, the pain can be so overwhelming that we need to use medical painkillers, because constant physical pain can be damaging and acute pain can be paralyzing. But what about heart-ache, when we are sorely missing our loved one who passed away? According to the Holmes-Rahe Scale, the stress impact of the death of a loved one is the greatest of all traumas (specifically your spouse or child, and for a child, the death of a parent). Medication is something that was developed using our God-given gifts, so it is permissible and sometimes even essential. But how should we go about using it?

When distress threatens to overwhelm you, sleep simply eludes you, or depression makes your life dangerously dark, it would be wise for you to seriously consider getting medical help. See it as a gift from God. However, if it becomes an escape in the long run—when medication (or alcohol) becomes a way of numbing your pain—then you must do what Jesus did and refuse to take it.

Jesus endured more pain than is humanly possible, but the prize for enduring that pain was so great that He did not want to use any form of anesthesia.

Medication can help you through the hardest times, but don't ever feel pressured to take it. Write down the possible advantages and disadvantages of using medication. Do not try to do it alone, pray about it and also speak to your doctor about it.

_____

_____

_____

_____

_____

_____

_____

_____

_____

_____

_____

_____

_____

_____

_____

_____

Lord, sometimes my pain is just overwhelming. It never ceases. I can't sleep anymore. I need Your help and relief. Please show me what the best option is for me. Please send reliable helpers my way. Help my doctor to be an instrument in Your hand. Amen.

20

If Only I...

"And He will answer, 'I tell you the truth, when you refused to help the least of these my brothers and sisters, you were refusing to help Me.'" (Matthew 25:45 NLT)

The things that we failed to do can be just as bad as the wrong things we did do. This is evident in Jesus' description of the final judgment. He condemns people for not helping the hungry, the sick, strangers and so forth. These people in Matthew 25 did nothing wrong, but in doing nothing, they also erred.

Sometimes the things we did not do but wish we had done can cause enormous regret. "I wish I had told him that I loved him. I wish I had done more for my loved one when they were still here. I wish I had helped her more when she was going through a hard time. I wish..."

But when someone has died, it is too late. Then your own guilt condemns you. The most bitter tears are cried when we mourn the hours we wasted. Jesus offers forgiveness—for regret and self-reproach, too. Even the Jesus followers in Matthew 25 sometimes overlooked someone, but because Jesus was in their hearts, they were more attentive to others' needs. The people He condemned were, however, blind to the needs of others because Jesus was never in their thoughts. They were condemned not for their negligence, but rather for their unbelief. Having Jesus in your heart makes all the difference.

Tell Jesus about everything that you failed to do for your loved one that makes you cry now. Do it again and again until the realization dawns on you: *Jesus has forgiven me, so I can forgive myself.*

It is hard to move on knowing that there are things you should have said or done, but failed to do. Write down some of those things below, then take all your regrets to God and experience His forgiveness.

_____

_____

_____

_____

_____

_____

_____

_____

_____

_____

_____

_____

_____

_____

_____

_____

_____

_____

_____

_____

_____

_____

Lord, You know all my deepest regrets. I wish I could go back and make things right, but I can't! Forgive me! I know that because of Your great love, You forgive at once but I am still struggling to forgive myself. Please keep helping me until I am finally able to do it. Amen.

Rise above
the Darkness

When our days become dreary
with low-hovering clouds of despair,
and when our nights become darker
than a thousand midnights,
let us remember that there is
a creative force in this universe,
working to pull down
the gigantic mountains of evil,
a power that is able
to make a way out of no way
and transform dark yesterdays
into bright tomorrows.

– Martin Luther King, Jr.

21

Write a Psalm

Why, my soul, are you downcast? Why so disturbed within me? Put your hope in God, for I will yet praise Him, my Savior and my God. (Psalm 42:11 NIV)

Some of the psalms can be pretty confusing. They hardly ever describe a single emotion. One verse is sad, one triumphant, the next pleading. That is why we enjoy reading the Psalms. And that is also why you should write your own psalm.

But before you start writing, think about what you can write about. We often think that we are only allowed to write beautiful, faith-filled, comforting or triumphant words. We refrain from writing any questions expressing doubt, or words that could be seen as being rebellious or hopeless. However, you have permission (the same permission the writers of the Book of Psalms had when they wrote it) to write down an honest account of all your confused thoughts.

What will happen while you write? Your feelings will start to change. Many of the psalms start out complaining and crying, but end in peace and faith. It is as if the writing process transforms feelings.

A more modern word for writing a psalm may be "journaling". It is a technique where you simply write down everything that goes through your mind, without stopping and without trying to organize your thoughts. You are simply unloading (or brain dumping). Before long, you will realize that you really did unload, because your load will be so much lighter.

Go ahead and write down your own psalm. Just write, it doesn't have to be neat or logical. Simply write down whatever pops into your mind.

_____

_____

_____

_____

_____

_____

_____

_____

_____

_____

_____

_____

_____

_____

_____

_____

_____

_____

_____

Heavenly Father, thank You for Your Word with so many honest psalms in it. It gives me the courage to be honest, too. I am going to write whatever is in my mind and heart. Will You please read through it with me afterwards and help me to make sense of it all? Please give me Your clarity, Lord. Amen.

22

Eternity Together

*For the Lord Himself will come down from heaven…and the
dead in Christ will rise first. After that, we who are still alive and
are left will be caught up together with them in the clouds to meet
the Lord in the air. And so we will be with the Lord forever. Therefore
encourage one another with these words. (1 Thessalonians 4:16-18 NIV)*

God created us to be eternal beings. His love for us is so great that He does not want the people He created to ever cease to exist. Love does not want to lose anyone. And that is why He offers us that same privilege and grace—to one day see our loved ones again. But when?

If we're truly honest, we would prefer no separation at all. The reality of your loved one's death, which you must deal with for the rest of your life here on earth, is terrible. That is why our heart's desire is to see each other again as soon as possible.

But all we have is the assurance that we will meet again, we don't know when it will happen. And that is because eternity does not have dates. Eternity is without time, outside of time. It is an indescribable place outside of time and space, but *with* God.

The only thing that we can do while we are still here on earth is to ask God to transform our impatience into excitement. Ask Him to remind you of the good times you had together, and to help you be excited about the perfect eternity that awaits.

How comforting it is to know that we will see our loved ones again! Write down some of the most precious memories you have of your loved one below.

_____

_____

_____

_____

_____

_____

_____

_____

_____

_____

_____

_____

_____

_____

_____

_____

Our Father in heaven, thank You for wanting us in heaven with You. We cannot imagine what it will be like, because eternity is incomprehensible. We are looking forward to it, though. Amen.

23

Made Beautiful

He will take our weak mortal bodies and change them into glorious bodies like His own, using the same power with which He will bring everything under His control. (Philippians 3:21 NLT)

In our eyes, very few things here on earth match the beauty of our loved ones. Our love casts every child or spouse in a light that makes them even more stunning than the winners of beauty pageants. Of course, the human body is such an astonishing miracle that every body and every face deserves to win a beauty competition. This biological miracle certainly deserves the first prize.

But our bodies are not really as "beautiful" as we might think. Our loved ones are covered in wrinkles, and come in weird shapes and sizes—even the beauties. Not to mention what happens when we start getting older! Our loved ones also have all kinds of quirks with peculiar mannerisms, habits and personalities.

So, we are very grateful that the Lord looks at us through the lens of love and that we are beautiful in His eyes. We are even more grateful that He will make us *truly* beautiful in eternity, where we will have a glorified body.

Will we be able to recognize each other if we are all so stunningly beautiful? God's creativity is so boundless that He will make each one of His children recognizable and beautiful. How wonderful it is to imagine how gorgeous our family will be—beautiful for His pleasure.

We can only imagine what everything will look like in heaven one day. Write down what you think it will be like.

_____

_____

_____

_____

_____

_____

_____

_____

_____

_____

_____

_____

_____

_____

_____

_____

_____

_____

_____

Lord, I sometimes wonder what it will be like to have a glorified body. That is why I am very excited about being with You in heaven one day. I praise You for that wonderful prospect. Amen.

24

A Heavenly Photo Album

Then I saw a great white throne and Him who
was seated on it...And I saw the dead, great
and small, standing before the throne, and
books were opened. Another book was opened,
which is the book of life. (Revelation 20:11-12 NIV)

When a loved one dies, our photo albums become some of our most prized possessions. It is a way to cherish memories and look back with gratitude. Photos may only capture a single moment of all the memories stored in our minds, and yet they are wonderfully alive.

We all have a kind of photo album in heaven, too. When all people stand before God one day, a book will be opened for each and every one of us. It sounds interesting, but also a little intimidating. Because that book will contain *everything*—your entire life with all its beauty and bloopers. So, it may bring with it shame and embarrassment, too.

Fortunately, the Book of Life will be opened soon after that. All the names of the people who believe in Jesus Christ are recorded in this Book. It is a Book of grace, because God accepts us not based on our own merit, but solely based on our faith and Jesus' grace. Without this Book, we would have been judged according to what we had done, and we would probably be turned away due to our mistakes and shortcomings.

So, we should be grateful for our photo albums, but even more so for this Book of grace.

Write down what goes through your mind when you look at photos of your loved one. You may even decide to share some memories with friends or family and soothe some of your heartache in that way.

Heavenly Father, I sometimes worry about what might be written in my book in heaven. There are surely things recorded in there that I am ashamed of. I actually wish that that book will never be opened. So, I want to ask You to erase the mistakes and sins. I ask that in Jesus' Name. Amen.

25

Going Home

"My Father's house has many rooms; if that were not so, would I have told you that I am going there to prepare a place for you? And if I go and prepare a place for you, I will come back and take you to be with Me that you also may be where I am." (John 14:2-3 NIV)

Maybe we should say that we are going home rather than we are going to heaven. Some place "among the stars" has a very different feeling to "home", which is where we belong.

Jesus gives His disciples a new future. In those days, the general understanding of life after death was the underworld—a place void of all hope and joy. But then He gives them a route to follow and a place. Of course, the house He refers to is also used figuratively, just like the New Jerusalem, Paradise or the New Earth.

But calling it His "Father's house" is very special. It does indeed have "many rooms", arguably more than the biggest hotel imaginable. But it is a home, where we are welcome, where we do not need to pay, and where our loved ones are at home with us. There is a special room prepared with your name on the door.

It makes sense that believers often talk about going home—particularly when they are enduring a lot of suffering. No matter how much they love those who will have to remain here for now, they long to experience heaven, and to be free from earthly pain and suffering. So, amid our own sadness, we can rejoice about our loved one's homecoming and know that our own places have already been prepared for us.

How wonderful it is to know that our place in heaven has already been prepared! Write down what you want to say to your loves ones when you meet them again.

_____

_____

_____

_____

_____

_____

_____

_____

_____

_____

_____

_____

_____

_____

_____

Heavenly Father, thank You for the Father's house, our heavenly home. Thank You for the many rooms and especially for mine. Death seems a lot less terrifying now. I am comforted by the thought that my loved one has finally come home to You! Amen.

26

Sending Messages

"…besides, there is a great chasm separating us.
No one can cross over to you from here, and no one
can cross over to us from there." (Luke 16:26 NLT)

Sometimes we have this burning desire in our hearts to have just *one* last conversation with our loved one. Surely, such a conversation will calm your pain and might help bring you closure.

Unfortunately, some people become so desperate that they approach swindlers who claim that they are able to convey messages beyond the grave. It usually costs a lot of money…and you will be wasting every single cent of it. In fact, instead of bringing people peace, it usually upsets them even more.

There is, however, a healthier method. You can write a letter to your loved one. This letter can, of course, never be delivered. But remember: You are writing the letter for *your own* sake, not your loved one's. Your loved one is already with God where there is complete joy and peace—and no amount of communication from your side will change that.

Writing such a letter can be very valuable. If you pen down the thoughts racing through your mind, the writing process will bring greater calmness. It is a good way to get everything that is in your heart out and onto paper, and it also helps to find closure. Write as many long letters as you feel you need to until you have said everything you wanted to.

Are there still things you feel you need to say in order to find closure? Go ahead and write them down here.

_____

_____

_____

_____

_____

_____

_____

_____

_____

_____

_____

_____

_____

_____

_____

_____

_____

Our Shepherd, my heart is restless. There are so many things racing through my mind, so many things I wish I had said. I know that it is not possible for me to have a conversation with my loved one, so I will write. I am asking for Your peace to envelop me as I write my heart out. Lead my wandering thoughts to green pastures and quiet waters. Amen.

27

Celebrating Birthdays

What shall we say about such wonderful things as these?
If God is for us, who can ever be against us?
No, despite all these things, overwhelming victory is
ours through Christ, who loved us. (Romans 8:31, 37 NLT)

Celebrating birthdays was not a biblical custom. We do, how-ever, read about Herod celebrating his birthday (see Matthew 14:6), but it only serves as a backdrop for John the Baptist's death. For modern Christians, however, birthdays are celebrations of joy and gratitude. We express our happiness about a loved one's life and we thoroughly enjoy every birthday.

For many people, the birthday of a loved one who is no longer there is extremely hard, especially that first birthday. They often wonder what to do with themselves on that day.

One option is to use that day to commemorate your loved one. Were they a good person, happy, a believer? What is everyone's take on your loved one's life? Involve everyone who loved them, but don't force anyone to participate if they don't want to. Who remembers what? When you spend time together, talking about a loved one, even about the sad memories, it does help to some-what ease the heartache.

Because none of us are ever completely good and constantly happy, we can find comfort in the words of Romans 8: God is always on our side and we have already gained the victory through Him. So, we know that in heaven there may not be a birthday celebration, but there will surely be a celebration of a surpassing victory.

Do you think such a day of commemoration will be a good way for you and your family and friends to celebrate the life of your loved one? Write down a few things that you would like to do on such a day. Remember that it may include sad memories, too.

_____

_____

_____

_____

_____

_____

_____

_____

_____

_____

_____

_____

_____

_____

_____

Lord, I can still remember all the birthdays that we thoroughly enjoyed celebrating together. I remember the children's parties, the teenager parties and the adult get-togethers. This year, there will be none of that, but we *remember*. This year, please give us the gift of precious memories. Amen.

28

Like Grass

*All people are like grass, and all their faithfulness
is like the flowers of the field...But now, this is what the
Lord says—"Do not fear, for I have redeemed you; I have
summoned you by name; you are Mine." (Isaiah 40:6, 43:1 NIV)*

Unfortunately, cemeteries are often neglected. We want a place that is neat and that shows respect, and that is also beautiful, peaceful and quiet. But then we find it unkept with weeds and overgrown grass.

"All people are like grass." That overgrown grass between the graves may be here today and gone tomorrow, without a trace. That is when we realize that our loved one is gone, too. But there are some traces of them still here like the granite tombstone, which does not decay. When one looks at the older parts of the cemetery, it is obvious that those people have been forgotten even though their names are still there.

Isaiah's grace-filled words remind us that God's grass-people are never nameless. Even though we are as perishable as grass, He called us by name. That name engraved on the tombstone, which may be forgotten by many, is never forgotten by God. He calls to you and says in love, "You belong to Me!" So, even though you—a person like grass—may be washed away by a river or burnt away by fire (see Isaiah 43:2), you will be remembered and your life will not simply disappear.

God's enormous and eternal love ensures that you will also keep existing for all time. God will never forget us. The loved ones who live on in your memory are remembered even more vividly by Him.

Describe your visit to the gravesite of your loved one. Remember that this is not the final resting place. Heaven is our final destination.

_____

_____

_____

_____

_____

_____

_____

_____

_____

_____

_____

_____

_____

_____

_____

_____

_____

_____

Father, I realize more than ever before that our lives are like grass. But I know that You hold us in Your hand. I find rest in You. Amen.

29

Forgive and Forget

*"But I tell you that anyone who is angry with a brother
or sister will be subject to judgment…This is how My
heavenly Father will treat each of you unless you forgive
your brother or sister from your heart." (Matthew 5:22, 18:35 NIV)*

There are instances when a person is not sad about someone
who passed away, but angry at him or her. Sometimes people
hurt you so deeply that you simply can't forgive them. Even the best
people also have flaws that you can't simply overlook, or so easily
forget about.

How can you forgive someone who is no longer here to offer
an apology, or with whom you can't talk things out? In such a
case, forgiveness is a one-sided matter and does not depend on
an apology. So, you must work through it on your own and make
a conscious decision to forgive.

The choice to forgive starts when you stand before Jesus. When
you are standing before Him, you can see that you were indeed
often the victim, but that you are not innocent either, you also
treated others badly at times. You need to be forgiven, too. Only
then can you shift your attention and realize that we are all in need
of grace. Because you have received forgiveness and grace, you
must extend the same to others, too.

It will not necessarily be a quick or easy process, but at least now
you have taken the first step away from anger and resentment.

Are you struggling to forgive a loved one, or are you the one in need of forgiveness? Write down what you need forgiveness for below. Also write down what you need to forgive others for. Then take your list to God.

_____

_____

_____

_____

_____

_____

_____

_____

_____

_____

_____

_____

_____

God of mercy, I admit that I have often struggled to forgive others, but right now I am finding it even harder. It is as if I am unable to forget another's faults. Please cleanse my mind with Your water of forgiveness. Cleanse me of my own sin, too. And show me how You have cleansed that "guilty" person as well. Amen.

30

Seventy Times Seven

Then Peter came to Him and asked, "Lord, how often
should I forgive someone who sins against me?
Seven times?" "No, not seven times," Jesus replied,
"but seventy times seven!" (Matthew 18:21-22 NLT)

*H*ave you ever considered that Matthew 18:22 might mean that we are supposed to forgive the *same* sin as many times as seventy times seven?

When you make the choice to forgive, it often happens that the painful event plays out in your mind again and again. It resurfaces and you can't help but to think about it again, after all, forgiveness does not cause amnesia. When it comes up again, you must choose to forgive once more and to let go of all vengeful thoughts. So, you might need to choose to walk away from your supposed right to be angry as many times as seventy times seven.

But how does one do that? Firstly, by deliberately trying to remember and not to forget. Make a list of everything that your loved one did that hurt you. Try to write it down in as much detail as possible. You may also want to speak to a counsellor or a wise helper about it. And then, when you start feeling angry again, pray about it. Ask the Lord to take away your pain, to help you surrender your anger, and to help you forgive completely. It is a process that you might just have to repeat as many times as seventy times seven.

Is there an event from your past that still evokes anger in you? Write it down below and ask the Lord to help you forgive again and again. Also decide whether you need to speak to a counsellor or a wise helper about it.

_____

_____

_____

_____

_____

_____

_____

_____

_____

_____

_____

_____

_____

_____

_____

_____

Heavenly Father, I am seemingly unable to quench the anger I feel because I was so deeply hurt. And I don't really feel like remembering or reliving it to be honest. But it constantly pops up and spoils my good days. That is why I am asking You to help me to forgive as many times as is necessary, so that I can easily put a stop to the vengeful thoughts when they come up again. Amen.

God Is with Me

I know, Lord,

that You do not lead me *around* sorrow—

but *through* it.

Even though I pass through

the depths of darkness

and it feels like

I cannot find Your hand,

I am not afraid,

because You are with me.

— *Jörg Zink*

31

Finding Peace

Do not be anxious about anything, but in every situation, by prayer and petition, with thanksgiving, present your requests to God. And the peace of God, which transcends all understanding, will guard your hearts and your minds in Christ Jesus. (Philippians 4:6-7 NIV)

Peace dissipates when your sorrow is deep. Peace of mind specifically is very rare when you are in mourning. During such times, peace in its fullest sense, the feeling that everything is in order—is almost unattainable, because due to the loss of your loved one, your life is *not* in order.

Attaining peace of mind surely feels impossible. Quite the opposite is actually true: You experience distress, sadness, pain, powerlessness, anger...That is not peace! And then the promise in Philippians 4:7 feels like an impossibility. In fact, it feels like a lack of peace that transcends all understanding. So, how can you find peace?

Just before the promise in verse 7, we are given a method. We have to tell God about everything we need. It means that every prayer, every conversation with Him, will bring you one step closer to that peace. Prayer activates God's power, which will make your petitions a reality.

Of course, a single prayer will not secure immediate peace. But every conversation with God brings more calmness. You might even lose the peace of mind that you experience at one stage, but you will surely regain it—that is the promise.

What are the things that you need to get off your chest before you can experience peace? Tell God about it.

_____

_____

_____

_____

_____

_____

_____

_____

_____

_____

_____

_____

_____

_____

_____

_____

_____

_____

_____

Lord, may I please name each item on my long list of concerns? I want to say it out loud so that it feels more like I am casting my burdens onto You. Will You then please give me peace of mind? Amen.

32

Why, Lord?

*Why do You hide Your face and forget
our misery and oppression? (Psalm 44:24 NIV)*

People often say that we should have faith like a child and not question the Lord at all. You must simply accept whatever trials and tribulations come your way. But that is wrong. In fact, children constantly ask questions, much more so than adults do.

So, go ahead and ask the Lord why this is happening to you in your time of tribulation. If we are not allowed to ask questions, even seemingly rebellious and offensive questions, then many of the psalms should be taken out of the Bible, because the Book of Psalms is filled with such questions and honest conversations with God.

In the Bible, the why-questions have much more to do with the heart than the mind. You do want an explanation, but the questions are more so expressing what is in your heart. They show that you are very upset—for whatever reason. It is like a child's why-questions. Children are looking for an explanation that is understandable on their level, but they are simultaneously also looking for a sense of security. They often put more faith in the person providing the answer than the answer itself. So, a child may be quite content even if they get an answer that they do not understand simply because that answer came from a parent whom they trust.

That is why the answer we get when we ask why a loved one died is sufficient, because it is the Father who provides the answer.

Are you also grappling with why questions? Don't be afraid to pose those questions to God. Write down your questions below and take them to Him.

_____

_____

_____

_____

_____

_____

_____

_____

_____

_____

_____

_____

_____

_____

_____

_____

_____

_____

_____

Heavenly Father, I sometimes feel like I shouldn't ask so many questions. From now on help me to ask, "Where to now?" instead of just "Why?" or "Give me a reason." I know that will be much more helpful. Amen.

33

You Are Not Alone

*"Don't call me Naomi," she told them.
"Call me Mara, because the Almighty has made
my life very bitter. I went away full, but the LORD
has brought me back empty." (Ruth 1:20-21 NIV)*

Naomi lost three special people in her life: her husband and her two sons. But how could she be so blind to say, "I came back empty"? Could she not see the person standing right next to her and recognize that her life was not entirely empty? It seems that she overlooked Ruth; unable to see her as a loved one, a pillar of hope. She only realized what a gem this daughter-in-law of hers really was much later in the book. What had blinded Naomi to this truth in the initial chapters?

Sorrow can fixate your gaze on all the empty places and make you overlook all the full spaces around you. It is so easy to remain focused solely on the sadness. What other loved ones still surround you? Which people form part of your blanket of meaningful relationships? When you are overwhelmed with grief, you run the risk of overlooking everyone who is still in your life. Parents can easily "lose" their other children because they are so consumed with mourning their deceased child. A man or woman can also stop being a parent to their children when they have lost a spouse.

It is not always easy to look past your own pain but if you try, you'll see that your life is not entirely empty. Ask the Lord to help you really *see* each other, care for one another and look after one another.

Do you think that you may have overlooked people in your life because you were unable to look past your own pain? Make a list of everyone who is still in your life and reach out to them.

Almighty God, forgive me for focusing only on what I have lost. Open my eyes to see all the loved ones who are still with me. Help me to show them how much I love and appreciate them. Amen.

34

Sow Good Things

A man reaps what he sows…Let us not become weary in doing good, for at the proper time we will reap a harvest if we do not give up. Therefore, as we have opportunity, let us do good to all people, especially to those who belong to the family of believers. (Galatians 6:7, 9-10 NIV)

God gave each of us a specific number of years to live. And it is important to remember that we will be held accountable for the choices we make during that time.

So, it is imperative to not only decide *what* we will sow, but also *whether* we will sow. That is why we receive this significant invitation: Use the time you have left to sow good things.

We often hear this invitation at funerals and it is especially then that we are confronted with the uncertainty of the duration of our lives. It doesn't matter whether you are young or old, you either have a lot or very little time left. No-one knows. So, the question is: What will you do with that time?

The most valuable thing you can take away from any funeral is to *do more good*, especially for your loved ones. And you can start doing it immediately: Decide to frequently express your love and appreciation out loud, and to be aware of each one's specific needs. There is a wonderful promise linked to this: If you sow love, you will also reap love. By being kind to one another, you are preparing a harvest of a happy family. How much time we will have together remains uncertain, so we must keep sowing!

Are there some things that you would still like to do? Make a list of all of them—even if you don't have the courage to do it just yet.

_____

_____

_____

_____

_____

_____

_____

_____

_____

_____

_____

_____

_____

_____

_____

_____

_____

_____

_____

_____

Lord Jesus, I have wasted so much time in my life. I want to stop. Please help me to identify what I must do and open my eyes to instances where I can demonstrate love. Amen.

35

Nearer to God

Jacob awoke from his sleep and said, "Surely the LORD is in this place, and I wasn't even aware of it!" The next morning Jacob got up very early. He took the stone he had rested his head against, and he set it upright as a memorial pillar. Then he poured olive oil over it. He named that place Bethel (which means "house of God"). (Genesis 28:16, 18-19 NLT)

The hymn *Nearer My God, to Thee* is a moving song. When played at a funeral, it makes people feel both sad and calm. It makes us sad because the melody reminds us of the sorrow accompanying death and the final farewell and yet is also comforts us because it invites us to draw nearer to our great Comforter.

The song relates Jacob's dream and his experiences when he was fleeing from his enraged brother Esau. He wanders alone, rests his head on a stone, but then his dream brings him closer to God. He sees a ladder extending up into heaven and hears God's promise: "I am with you. I will protect you and I will bring you back to this land." In his most desperate moment, God drew nearer to him.

That is the comfort offered by this song. When you reach rock bottom, God *will* draw near to you. When you think you are too far gone that there is no help nor support left for you, God allows you to experience Him.

During your recent time of mourning, there were indeed divine moments. Maybe it was when you were listening to the trumpet sounds. Maybe it was a sunset or a conversation, or maybe a moment somewhere in nature. When you think back, you will realize that God was there with you. *That* is your Bethel.

How can you feel close to your loved one—through gardening, cooking a special meal, or volunteering at a shelter?

_____

_____

_____

_____

_____

_____

_____

_____

_____

_____

_____

_____

_____

_____

_____

_____

_____

_____

_____

_____

_____

Nearer, my God, to Thee; nearer to Thee! E'en though it be
a cross that raiseth me...still all my song shall be: nearer,
my God, to Thee, nearer, my God, to Thee; nearer to Thee!

36

Good and Evil

And we know that in all things God works for
the good of those who love Him, who have been
called according to His purpose. (Romans 8:28 NIV)

"Everything happens for a reason." Whenever people say this they usually mean that God had a plan right from the start and that He predetermined certain events to achieve some ideal goal. It could be a source of great comfort, especially when events just don't make any logical sense.

It can, however, also upset you greatly. When something terrible happens, it is upsetting to think that God ordained it. When millions of people perish in a world war, when a loved one is murdered or raped, it is unthinkable that God wanted something like that to happen. Thinking that it must have happened for a good reason also doesn't offer much comfort. Surely, the little good that could come from it will never outweigh the bad or justify the trauma.

Romans 8:28 says quite the opposite, though. It says that God possesses the power and love to take evil events, which were not His will, and transform them into something that doesn't destroy us, but rather brings forth something good.

We must, of course, do our part as well. Even if a cruel criminal were to murder our loved one, we must work through the trauma with God's grace so that it doesn't break us. Working through the trauma is necessary to turn the negative outcome of evil events into something good.

Take Romans 8:28 and fill in your own words: And we know that in (make a list of the bad things in your life) God works for the good of those who love Him, who have been called according to His purpose.

_____

_____

_____

_____

_____

_____

_____

_____

_____

_____

_____

_____

_____

_____

_____

_____

_____

_____

Heavenly Father, I sometimes struggle to cope with all the evil on earth. I yearn for Your will to be done here on earth as it is in heaven. So, I pray that You will take all the pain and suffering and evil, and turn it into something good. Help me to search for and work with You for a good outcome. Amen.

37

In God's Hands

*For I am convinced that neither death nor life,
neither angels nor demons, neither the present
nor the future, nor any powers, neither height nor
depth, nor anything else in all creation, will be able
to separate us from the love of God that is in
Christ Jesus our Lord. (Romans 8:38-39 NIV)*

The world we live in is riddled with many dangers. Romans 8 lists all the possible things that could seemingly tear a believer from God's hand. They are serious dangers: What if something happens in the future that makes us lose our faith, or what if evil powers attack us? It is precisely in the murky depths of despair after a loved one's death that we sometimes fear losing our faith.

But that is precisely why Romans 8 is such good news! The heavenly Father is holding our hand. He will not allow anything to tear us from His grip, nor will He allow us to tear ourselves loose. His love is simply too great to allow that.

This verse also offers consolation in the case of suicide. Some believers think that someone who has committed suicide can't go to heaven. But death, no matter how it happened, can never separate a believer from God. Jesus' grace does not depend on our last moments.

You can be at peace, convinced of God's everlasting hand holding you and your loved ones.

What a comfort it is to know that God will never let us go! Is there still any doubt or unbelief in your heart? Write it down below and then take it to God in prayer.

_____

_____

_____

_____

_____

_____

_____

_____

_____

_____

_____

_____

_____

_____

_____

_____

_____

_____

Lord, thank You for holding my hand with Your everlasting grip. I am sorry for sometimes acting like a naughty child who wants to go my own way. Yet You hold me tightly. Give me the power today to oppose any and all influences that want to tear me away from You. Amen.

38

New Habits

"A new command I give you: Love one another.
As I have loved you, so you must love one another.
By this everyone will know that you are My disciples,
if you love one another." (John 13:34-35 NIV)

*I*f the death of a loved one does not change you, nothing will ever change you. Suppose you want to change and you ask the Lord to show you how, what do you think He would say?

The answer will be plain and simple: Learn to love more. Focus more on loving your neighbor than yourself. Unfortunately, it is often true that things like success, possessions and our own experiences are higher up on our priority list than other people. In fact, society teaches us to rather focus on raking in money, possessions and achievements. That is why death is such a wake-up call as it helps us realize what is truly important in life.

John 13 actually demonstrates the method of achieving the ultimate success. If you set off a chain reaction of love, it leads to much greater success than a single achievement. Our constant demonstration of love cultivates a chain reaction of love all around us, which continues into the generations after us. Such a chain reaction of love will still be impressive hundreds of years down the line.

Jesus set off the ultimate chain reaction of love and 2,000 years later, it still makes the world a better place. You can do the same. Even amid your pain and suffering, you can learn to love more.

In which ways can you start to live out more love? Write them down while you thank Jesus for setting off the ultimate chain reaction of love.

Lord, our God, I yearn for more love. I really do want to demonstrate Your love to others—abundantly, freely. I want to be actively involved in Your love project here on earth. Please help me to be generous and spontaneous toward everyone who comes my way. Amen.

39

A Great Blessing

"Blessed are those who mourn,
for they will be comforted." (Matthew 5:4 NIV)

The Beatitudes contain some really strange promises. They often make something that seems like a bad thing sound like a blessing. In fact, it is specifically stated that a time of mourning can also be a blessed time. But how does that work?

It starts by realizing that a blessing is not necessarily always something that is nice and easy. The most satisfying moments in life are precisely those times when we had to give it our all to achieve something. A blessed life is not just a comfortable and easy life. Such a life will only make you lazy.

So, if you work through your pain, it will bring about blessing. That is the testimony of every believer several years after experiencing a disaster or trauma: I have become stronger. My faith has been purified. I am now living in a closer relationship with God and in greater dependence on Him. I am a better person.

How can you use this ripeness in ministry? Some of the most blessed ministries originated when people decided to help others in the area where they themselves had experienced the most pain. Maybe you can offer help to others who have also lost a loved one? Listen to your heart: You will feel prompted and then you will *want* to help those who need it.

The greatest blessing of all is the promise that you will also find comfort in the process. The best part of your ministry is being able to testify that even after grief you have been comforted and made whole again.

What is your testimony? In what ways have you changed? Can you think of someone you can comfort?

_____

_____

_____

_____

_____

_____

_____

_____

_____

_____

_____

_____

_____

_____

_____

_____

_____

_____

_____

Our Father, this last season has been difficult. Grief and suffering nearly overwhelmed me at times. I can, however, also see that I have grown. I am no longer the same. Help me to put this newfound experience and wisdom to meaningful use. Show me where I can help. Amen.

40

Life after Death

*"Look! God's dwelling place is now among the people,
and He will dwell with them. They will be His people,
and God Himself will be with them and be their God.
'He will wipe every tear from their eyes. There will be
no more death' or mourning or crying or pain, for the
old order of things has passed away." (Revelation 21:3-4 NIV)*

Every believer knows that there is life after death. Once we
have died, we will live with God forevermore.

Sometimes, people's grief after the death of a loved one is so
great that they lose the will to live here on earth. Their sorrow
convinces them that there is no life worth living after the loss of
their loved one. How does God restore your life here—a life that
includes joy, purpose and good times?

Look ahead. In our sorrow, we often think that this is how it will
be forever, that we will always experience such intense pain and
no joy. But try to look a few years into the future. The Lord *will* dry
your tears. He will wipe them away day after day; the sense of loss
will eventually fade and have less of an affect on you. In that time,
it will not be time that heals all wounds, but the Lord as *He* heals
all your wounds.

Then look ahead even further—to Revelation 21. That is life
after death in all its fullness—with God, with one another, without
tears and death separating loved ones.

Right now, we are *close* to God; then we will be *with* God.

Does sorrow still overwhelm you? Then ask God to reveal to you those things that you can get excited about. Write them down below.

_____

_____

_____

_____

_____

_____

_____

_____

_____

_____

_____

_____

_____

_____

_____

_____

Dear Lord, I must admit that during this past season there were times when I lost my will to live. The sorrow and loneliness drained all the joy from my life. Thank You for giving me small portions of joy once again. Today, please reduce my moments of sadness and amplify my moments of joy. Amen.

A Deeper Awareness of Grace

I will always want the ones I lost back again.
I long for them with all my soul.
But I still celebrate the life I have found
because they are gone.
I have lost, but I have also gained.
I lost the world I loved,
but I gained a deeper awareness of grace.
That grace has enabled me
to clarify my purpose in life
and rediscover the wonder
of the present moment.

– Jerry Sittser

Cherish Your Memories

How old was your loved one when they passed away? Are you satisfied with the portion of life measured out for them? It is often easier to be satisfied with their portion if they lived a long and fulfilling life. It is, however, very difficult to be satisfied when someone died an untimely death with so many years of life still ahead of them, so many years that you looked forward to spending together. It is also more difficult to feel satisfied if someone's life was full of suffering.

The truth is that life is a mixture of beautiful and ugly, good and bad, and easy and hard times for all of us. We also know that when God is at the center of our lives, it is more than just good enough—it is wonderful. Healthy mourning is when we are able to recognize the good *and* bad, and accept all of it. Then we are able to smile through the tears as we reflect on the life of a loved one, and we rejoice in the Lord for that person's presence and influence in our lives.

It may not feel like it right now, but you will get through this time of sorrow with the Lord's love and support. Do not force anything if you don't feel ready for it, but also don't get stuck in your sorrow. Make God part of every step of this process. You have His promise: He will always be with you and He will never let you go.

When you feel up to it, consider writing down your loved one's life story. Buy a special book specifically for that purpose. Look at old photographs. Walk through every season, don't skip a thing. In doing so you will learn that the good and bad make up a wonderfully full life with the Lord.

"*Very truly* I tell you,
you will weep and mourn
while the world *rejoices*.
You will grieve,
but your grief will turn to *joy*.
So with you:
Now is your time of grief,
but I will *see you again*
and you will *rejoice*,
and no one will
take away *your joy*."

JOHN 16:20, 22 NIV

About the Author

Dr. Henk Gous is a pastor and has held many leadership positions in the church. Counseling, preaching and youth work have been at the forefront of his ministry. He enjoys cycling and long walks in nature.